GARY JONES

Vilnius

First edition

This book was professionally typeset on Reedsy.
Find out more at reedsy.com

Contents

Introduction

Not many people have heard of Vilnius, the capital of Lithuania, and for the time being, that's forgivable. After all, on paper, it's just a small city with a population of a little over 500,000. But guess what: if you keep reading for the next few minutes or, this small, unheard-of, Lithuanian city just might become your next travel destination.

Vilnius is one of the last few remaining medieval cities in Europe. It is a city that boasts the harmonious balance of old and new, country and city, tradition and innovation. The city is also a UNESCO Heritage site that boasts of well-preserved architectural works with Baroque, Gothic, and Renaissance influences. It is also the major economic center of Lithuania, accounting for almost 40% of the country's GDP.

With its cobblestone streets and pastel-colored medieval buildings, Vilnius is a city seemingly plucked out from a fairy-tale. It's reminiscent of simpler times, but Vilnius isn't a city of empty nostalgia. People come for the postcard, picture-perfect panorama, but they stay for something more complex.

A deeper look into Vilnius shows that their art, history, culture, and people haven't always been picture-perfect. Oppression, adversity, and violence can either make or break a city, but it made Vilnius what it is today.

It is a city that had to fight for its freedom to practice their religion, for the freedom to speak their own language, and for the freedom to simply live. And through that, Vilnius has developed a strong sense of cultural identity. It is self-realized, independent, and authentic; it doesn't take cues and it doesn't follow trends. It's a city that knows who it is, and takes pride in it.

1

Basic Information

Official language: Lithuanian

Emergency number: 112

Currency: Euro and Lithuanian litas. You can exchange currencies in the airport, currency exchange offices in bus and train stations, and banks.

Tourism information: Visit the official website of Vilnius tourism at http://vilnius-tourism.lt/en/ Walking and sightseeing tours, maps, city cards, and audio guides are also available there. Tourist information centers can also be found at the following locations:

Pilies g. 2, Vilnius 01124, Lithuania. Open every day, 9am - 6pm

Didžioji g. 31, Vilnius 01128, Lithuania. Open every day, 9am - 1pm, 2pm - 6pm

Rodūnios kl. 2, Vilniaus tarptautinis oro uostas, Vilnius 02189, Lithuania. Open every day, 9am - 7pm

Basic etiquette: Lithuanians appreciate honesty, modesty, and formality. The traditional greeting is a firm handshake, followed by minimal small talk. The basic rule of thumb is respect: don't arrive late, don't interrupt conversations, and don't abuse a person's generosity.

Tipping: Tipping is a new practice in Vilnius cafe, bars, and restaurants. A 10% tip is standard.

2

Vilnius, a History

According to legend, the city of Vilnius started as a king's dream. In 1322, Gediminas, the Grand Duke of Lithuania who would later become King, was visited by a vision in his sleep. The dream was of an ironclad wolf, perched on top of a hill, howling with the force of a thousand of its kin. For guidance, he turned to his priest, Lizdeika. Lizdeika divined his dream, and told him that the ironclad wolf was the symbol of a city that Gediminas is destined to build. According to the priest, that city will become Lithuania's capital, and its success and glory will astound even those in the farthest reaches of the world. Following this divination, Vilnius was soon founded.

Lithuania's history has been tumultuous, to say the least. In the past fifty years alone, it has suffered through foreign invasions, uprisings, territorial disputes, civil wars, and was witness to both world wars. In 1991, Vilnius was occupied by the Soviet Union. This was a violent and destructive period - places of worship were desecrated, historic statues were replaced, and cultural wonders were looted. Citizens were expelled from their homes, and were forced to abandon their language and religion. Many were killed when they resisted.

In response to these atrocities, the citizens of Vilnius came together to form a resistance movement called Sąjūdis. In March 11, 1990, the people of Lithuania declared their independence, which the Soviets did not peacefully accept. They responded with blockades, cutting off the citizens' access to food, water, heating, and electricity. In the name of the resistance, many died and more were injured. This lasted for 18 months, and then, because of the unwavering resistance from this small, war-torn city in Lithuania, the Soviet Union's collapse began.

The country's declaration of independence brought about the wide-scale rehabilitation of the city. There was a lot of work to do; Lithuania, compared to its European neighbors, was lagging behind in terms of financial and economic growth.

But Vilnius, as the capital of the country, paved the way for restoration efforts. Resources were replenished, small shops were rebuilt, and churches were reopened. The rapid rise of Vilnius soon began to attract foreign investors. High-rise buildings, skyscrapers, and modern apartments were began to pop up throughout the city come the late 1990's.

Old Town is not only the oldest part of the city capital, it is also the city's heart and soul. Through its architecture, it reflected the wealth of cultures and influences that the country had - gothic, renaissance, baroque, and neoclassical. However, many of these buildings were severely damaged by raids, looting, fire, and illegal squatters. In 1997, Vilnius turned its rehabilitative efforts onto Old Town. Its historical buildings were restored, the hotels were reopened, and residential buildings were built. For the first time in fifty years, Vilnius was becoming a tourist destination once again.

Brick by brick, Lithuania was slowly restored. In 2001, just ten years after its declaration of independence, Vilnius was declared a modern European city. Despite its blood-stained history, or perhaps because of it, Vilnius has a strong sense of cultural identity. Today, in this era of peace and prosperity, Vilnius and its people invite you to experience it with them.

3

When to Go

Lithuania's climate is semi-continental: its summers are slightly rainy and comfortably hot, while its winters are brutally long and bitingly cold. But every seasoned traveller (no pun intended) knows there's no such thing as "the best time" to visit a country. Each season brings something different to the table, and it's just a matter of finding out what suits your interests the best.

December - February

Admittedly, "brutally long and bitingly cold" isn't the best way to convince anyone to go to Vilnius during winter. Not everyone can endure a harsh Baltic winter, but those who can, will be pleased to know that the December chill transforms Vilnius. Trakai's lakes become frozen, Tauras hills become skiable, and the beautiful medieval city looks magical against the white backdrop of the snow. Winter ends in a flurry of events, such as the Lithuanian Centennial and Užgavėnės.

The average high is 28°F and the average low is 20°F. Include warm clothes in your packing list: heavy coat, thick sweater, scarves, thermal underwear, and long socks. Also bring boots, gloves, umbrellas, and other winter accessories.

March - April

Anywhere in the world, the end of winter is always warmly welcomed, and it is especially true in Baltic countries. Spring in Vilnius is celebrated with art, music, and festivities like the Kaziukas Fair, Street Music Day, Užupis Independence Day, St. Patrick's Day, and St. Casimir's Fair.

The average high is 46°F and the average low is 32°F. In recent years, spring came a few weeks late. Early March is warmer than winter but layers of snow still haven't thawed. If you're interested to see the city in all its springtime glory, it is best to book your trip for the last two weeks of April. Days are clear and comfortably warm, but expect slightly rainy nights. Pack light cotton shirts and breathable pants, and don't forget to bring an umbrella.

May - August

In summer, Vilnius takes advantage of the sun and the long days. It is when the city is at its most active; locals especially enjoy playing sports or being out and about in nature. Summer in Vilnius has its fair share of running events, too – including the Women's Run, Trail Run, and XV Danske Bank Vinius Marathon, to name a few. If you're looking for something more laidback and festive, perhaps you would enjoy the Vilnius Burger Fest, Culture Night, or riding a hot air balloon.

The average high is 68°F and the average low is 50°F. Compared to other countries in Europe, Vilnius in summer can still be cool. Think layers: cardigans, comfortable tees, and jeans. Also bring an umbrella, a pair of sunglasses, and a pair of walking shoes.

September - November

If you truly want to have an immersive experience in Vilnius culture, visit the city in autumn. This season in particular is jam-packed with festivities like the Vilnius Beer Festival, New Circus Weekend, Loftas Fest, Autumn Equinox, and Vilnius City Fiesta. The crisp autumn air also encourages a stroll in the city or a hike in the outskirts. Whatever activity you choose, you'll be greeted by a view of the picturesque city, splashed with specks of red, yellow, green, and brown.

The average high is 43°F and the average low is 34°F. September and October are warm and sunny months, but November is colder. Pack accordingly; bring layers, wool sweaters, cardigans, and light pants. Wear closed comfortable shoes and, as always, don't forget your umbrella.

Events

To spice up your visit, here is a list of Vilnius' most famous public events, festivals, and fairs.

Užgavėnės (February)

Užgavėnės, the Lithuanian Mardi Gras, is celebrated on the seventh week before Easter. The festival symbolizes the eternal conflict between good and evil, spring and winter, Lašininis and Kanapinis. The city celebrates by burning an effigy of winter, masquerade dances, and eating pancakes.

St. Casimir's weekend (March)

St. Casimir Fair is one of the oldest traditions of Vilnius, dating back to as early as the 17th century.

During the fair, the Vilnius town square, streets, and markets explode with folk arts and crafts like handcrafted trinkets, woven clothes, special coins, festive dishes and Casimir's Heart cookies.

Held on the weekend after Saint Casimir's Day, Kaziukas Fair celebrates the coming of spring. During the fair, expect plenty of music, various spectacles, theatrical street performances, traditional Lithuanian food, and Easter palms.

Vilnius Festival (June)

June in Vilnius is a classical music lover's dream. The International Vilnius Festival is a two-week long celebration of Lithuanian and foreign classical music. It features performances by the Lithuanian National Symphony Orchestra, Wroclaw Baroque Orchestra, Vienna Philharmonic Orchestra, and Quartetto di Cremona.

Vilnius Burger Fest (July)

Towards the end of July, the quest for the best burger in Lithuania begins. The Vilnius Burger Fest started a decade ago as a way to promote burgers and street food in Lithuania. Every year, the culinary festival astounds the city with a wide selection of experimental gourmet burgers.

Vilnius City Fiesta (September)

The Vilnius City Fiesta celebrates art in all forms - music, visual art, film, folk art, and more. Every year, over 300,000 people visit the festival to watch free artistic performances, live concerts, and exhibitions.

Christmas in Vilnius (December)

As a predominantly Christian country, Christmas is the most famous holiday in Vilnius. Christmas is a month-long celebration, starting with the lighting of the Vilnius Christmas Trees in the Town Square. Even the trains aren't immune to the holiday season. The elf-operated trains are painted candy cane colors and decorated with wreaths, ornaments, and Christmas lights. Other events include Vilnius Christmas Run, and Christmas Eve Mass, and New Year's Eve Fair.

4

Safety

Generally, Vilnius is a safe country. The streets may seem a little rough around the edges, but places like Old Town and Užupis are going through a rehabilitative, revitalizing time. Vilnius' streets are safe to walk in, even at night. All things considered, the precautions to take in Vilnius are no different from the ones you should remember when in metropolitan cities like New York or London. Here are some safety tips to follow to ensure a safe trip.

1 - As with any city capital, there is a small risk of petty theft, pick-pocketing, and tourist scams. Such incidents are likely to happen in busy streets, train and bus stations. Be vigilant. Locals tend to keep to themselves, so be wary of people who approach you out of the blue.

2 - When travelling, it is best to limit your drinking, especially when you're drinking alone. Violent crimes in Vilnius very commonly involve drunk individuals. Also note that driving under the influence is severely prohibited. It is punishable by imprisonment or thousands of euros in fines.

3 - Wear discreet, sensible clothes. For obvious reasons, newcomers are easy targets. To avoid being treated like a tourist, avoid looking like a tourist. Wear plain clothing to avoid unnecessary attention.

4 - Lithuania is relatively safe from natural disasters, but always bring an umbrella in case of rain.

5 - Know the emergency numbers and locations. Familiarize yourself with nearby hospitals and police precincts in case it comes in handy. Dial 112 in case of an emergency. If you have allergies or other medical conditions, wear your medic alert bracelet.

6 - At the moment, Lithuania is not as accepting of LGBT people as other Western countries are. Recent surveys have found that only 20% of Lithuanians approve of same-sex marriage. For safety reasons, public display of affection is not encouraged in gay couples.

7 – Use common sense. This is the most basic rule of traveling, and this is what the other rules are built upon. Don't flash the cash you're carrying, don't go into dark alleys, and don't ignore your gut feeling.

5

Transport

As a capital city, Vilnius is an easy city to get to and to get around in. Getting to Vilnius is possible by plane or train, and getting around in Vilnius is made convenient by the accessible and affordable public transportation system.

Getting to Vilnius

By plane

Direct transatlantic flights to Vilnius might be hard to come by, but connecting flights from other European cities can get you to Vilnius. Flights to Vilnius land at Vilnius International Airport, the only airport in the city. It is state-owned and is pretty bare-bones. However, it is only 6km away from the city and highly accessible via public transport.

From the airport, you can take a train, airport bus, minibus, or taxi to get to the city center.To get from the airport to the city via train, head to the train station. Purchase a ticket (€0.72) from the station ticket office. The travel time from the airport to the city is just 8 minutes.

The train is a convenient option for those who are travelling alone and travelling light. Vilnius trains run every day from 5:45am - 10pm.

To get from the airport to the city via airport bus, head towards the terminal exit. Turn left, then follow the signs to the bus stop. Travelling to the city via bus costs €1 and takes about 20 minutes.

This option is for those who have been to Vilnius before and are somewhat familiar with the area. Airport buses are operational from 5:25am - 10pm on weekdays, 6am - 10pm on weekends.

To get from the airport to the city via minibus, head towards the airport exit. Tickets cost €1.6, and the travel time is about 20 minutes. Given the limited luggage storage, minibuses are frequently used by lightly-packed solo travelers.

To get from the airport to the city via taxi, head to the airport exit. Lithuanian taxi drivers have been known to overcharge tourists, so be vigilant. Driving to the city should only take about 15-20 minutes and cost about €20.

This is a favorable option for those travelling with children, senior citizens, and disabled people. Taxis are available 24/7, so it's also suitable for those travelling at night.

Should you need any assistance, do not hesitate to go to the Vilnius Tourist Information Centre, located at the lobby of the arrival terminal.

Vilnius Airport (VNO)
   Rodūnios kl. 10A, Vilnius 02189, Lithuania

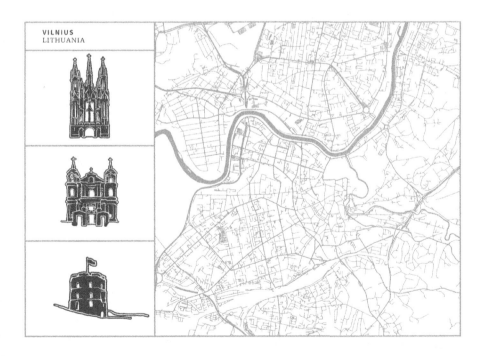

By train

If you are coming in from other cities in Lithuania, Poland, Belarus, or Russia, you can ride a direct train to Vilnius. The Vilnius Railway Station is centrally located and is near hotels, restaurants, and tourist attractions in Old Town.

For more information on schedule, routes, ticket costs, and other concerns, go to http://www.litrail.lt/

Train Website

Vilnius Railway Station
  Geležinkelio g. 22, Vilnius 02100, Lithuania

© *OpenStreetMap contributors*

Getting around Vilnius

Buses are the most popular mode of transportation in Vilnius. It is an affordable, accessible, and straightforward way to get around the city. For more details on schedules and bus stop locations, go to http://www.vilniusticket.lt/.

To use the bus, simply purchase a ticket from the driver for €1, then validate the ticket in the puncher. Alternatively, if you intend to ride the bus multiple times during your trip, you can purchase a Vilniečio kortelė or an electronic card. You can purchase a card by number of trips or number of days. To use the card, simply wave it in front of the yellow machine near the driver.

Cars are available for rent for as low as €15 per day. Renting is a sensible option if you wish to visit off-the-beaten-path locations unreachable by public transportation. However, if your destinations are limited to Old Town and nearby places, parking places are often limited so car rental may not be worth the hassle.

Taxis will get you wherever you need to go, but it can be expensive and risky. Alternatively, ride-sharing apps are also available in Vilnius. The advantages of ride-sharing apps include being able to track your ride and knowing the exact fare amount. However, the disadvantages are price surcharges – depending on traffic conditions, high demand, or booking time, the fare can increase by about 40%.

Bicycle

A cheap, easy and convenient way to see the city is to rent a bicycle. The city has a bike sharing system but there are also many private options available. You can find out more about the bike sharing at https://www.cyclocity.lt/en/ .

Bike Sharing
  Phone:+370 800 22 008

Vilnius Bike Tours
  Pylimo g. 31, Vilnius

+370 674 12123

6

Top Hotels

As a highly urbanized city, Vilnius also has a variety of high quality hotels that will suit different preferences and needs. The city has options for every tourist's consideration. No matter your budget, preferences, or group size, Vilnius has a place for you.

Hotel Panorama

Hotel Panorama is a contemporary three-star hotel situated in the middle of Old Town, just a few minutes away from Gate of Dawn, All Saints Church and Gediminas' Tower. Hotel Panorama might be mid-range in price, but it cuts no corners when it comes to comfort, cleanliness, and security. The on-site amenities include a bar, restaurant, lounge area, and casino. They also offer walking tours for a small fee.

A standard hotel room costs €42 per night and comes complete with a double bed, flat screen TV, and private toilet and bath. The 18 sqm room also has air-conditioning, heating, and free Wi-Fi. Also note that the hotel and the rooms are wheelchair-accessible.

You can find Hotel Panorama at Sodu g. 14, Vilnius Old Town, Vilnius 03211, Lithuania. Book a room by calling +370 5 233 8822.

Urbihop Hotel

Urbihop Hotel is a modern minimalist three-star hotel located in Viršuliškės, thirty minutes away from Old Town. It is a stone's throw away from popular shopping destinations, such as Panorama Shopping Mall and Akropolis Shopping and Entertainment Centre. The in-house restaurant offers local, international, and European cuisine. Other amenities include a spa, sauna, wellness centre, and fitness centre.

At €40 per night, you'll get a no-frills room, inclusive of a buffet breakfast. The 18 sqm room offers standard amenities: double bed, private shower and toilet, flat screen TV, heating, air-conditioner, and free Wi-Fi.

Urbihop Hotel is located at Ąžuolyno g. 7, Virsuliskes, Vilnius 07171, Lithuania. Contact the hotel at +370 5 233 8822 for more information.

City Hotels Algirdas

City Hotels Algirdas is a family-friendly four-star hotel located in New Town. The Scandinavian decor is elegant yet whimsical, classy yet welcoming. Its restaurant also offers excellent French cuisine and outdoor seating.

A family room in City Hotels Algirdas costs €95 per night. The 25 sqm room comes with a large double bed for the adults and a sofa bed for the kids. The family room includes amenities like a minibar, private bathroom, flat-screen TV with satellite channels, ironing facilities, heating, air-conditioning, and free Wi-Fi. The room is also soundproofed, non-smoking, and hypoallergenic.

Visit City Hotels Algirdas at Algirdo g. 24, Naujamiestis, Vilnius 03218, Lithuania. For questions and concerns, call +370 5 232 6650.

Radisson Blu Royal Astorija Hotel

Radisson Blu Royal Astorija Hotel is a five-star hotel centrally located in Old Town, dedicated to giving guests a luxurious experience without breaking the bank. The Radisson's decor exudes extravagance, from its Baroque facade, to the modern chic rooms, rejuvenating indoor pool, and fully-equipped fitness room. Its restaurant, Astorija Brassiere, offers classic and modern French cuisine with a view of the town square.

The standard guest room goes for €125 per night and it comes with free breakfast and access to the hotel's Health Club. The 20 sqm room is furnished with a double bed, flat screen television with cable and satellite channels, basic kitchen appliances, private toilet and bath, ironing facilities, and free Wi-Fi. The room is also air-conditioned and soundproofed, and it looks out to a scenic view of the city.

Radisson Blu Royal Astorija Hotel is at Didzioji g. 35/2, Vilnius Old Town, Vilnius 01128, Lithuania. Call +370 5 212 0110 to book a room.

B&B&B&B&B

B&B&B&B&B is a clean, comfortable hostel that aims to provide a satisfying experience to the budget-minded traveller. It's located right at the edge of Old Town, only six minutes away from the Vilnius bus and train station.

Its interiors are eye-catching - the furnishings are modern chic, well-lit and quite spacious. The hostel facilities are interesting, to say the least. The place has a lounge, bar, restaurant, entertainment zone, and an indoor skating park. Yes, you read the last part right! They even offer skateboarding lessons for a small fee.

They have private rooms and dormitories with 6, 8, 10, and 14 pax capacity. A private room costs €25 per night, and is furnished with a double bed, seating area, basic kitchen appliances, ironing facilities, and a shared bathroom. They also offer free Wi-Fi, which is rare at this price point.

B&B&B&B&B is located at Kauno g. 5, Naujamiestis, Vilnius 03215, Lithuania. Contact the hostel at +370 626 45614.

7

Top Landmarks

Vilnius is Lithuania's nucleus of religion, politics, culture, art, and science; thus, many of the iconic and significant tourist attractions can be found in the city. Here are the top 5 must-see tourist attractions in

Vilnius.

Church of St. Anne

Vilnius is one of the only remaining medieval cities in Northern Europe. What makes it truly remarkable is how much and how well medieval buildings are preserved. A prime example of this is the Church of St. Anne.

In the 14th century, the church was a simple place of worship made primarily out of wood. Since then, the Church of St. Anne has undergone many reconstructions, and the result is a breathtaking and harmonic composition of Flamboyant Gothic, neo-Gothic, Late Gothic, and Brick Gothic architecture.

Legend has it that Emperor Napoleon visited the church in 1812, and remarked that he wished to take the church in the palm of his hand, and take it home with him to Paris.

The Church of St. Anne is located at Maironio g. 8, Vilnius 01124, Lithuania.

Gate of Dawn

In 1503, ten city gates were built to fortify its defenses against Muscovite invaders. By 1805, only the Gate of Dawn remains, and to this day, it is intact, well-preserved, and reputable.

Over the years, The Gate of Dawn has gained historical, religious, and cultural significance because of the painting situated on top of the gate. It is a miraculous painting of the Blessed Virgin Mary, entitled "Our Lady of the Gate of Dawn." Religious artifacts like these are believed to bless passersby and wards off attackers. Legend has it that Our Lady of the Gate of Dawn even played a part in winning the Great Northern War of 1702. Such was its popularity that it warranted a visit and a sermon from Pope John Paul II in 1993.

Visit Gate of Dawn at Aušros Vartų g. 14, Vilnius 01303, Lithuania. It is open every day from 6am – 7pm.

Gediminas' Castle

King Gediminas built this castle and declared Vilnius as the capital of Lithuania. The tower has a small museum dedicated to honoring the castle's role in Lithuanian history, from 14th to 17th century. The castle also features an observation deck on top of the tower, where you will be greeted with a panoramic view of the city of Vilnius.

The castle is built on top of a small hill 40 meters high. You can enter through the funicular, or you can take the scenic route and walk uphill, which can take about 20 minutes.

Gediminas' Castle is located at Arsenalo g. 5, Vilnius 01143, Lithuania. It is open every day from 10am - 6pm. There is an entrance fee of €5 for adults.

Bernardine Gardens

The Bernardine Garden is a nine-hectare family-friendly public park just ten minutes away from Gediminas' Castle. The garden serves as Vilnius' oasis - a perfect spot for tourists who want to take a break after a packed day.

It is also a destination in its own right. Here, you can have a picnic, take a stroll in the gardens, play chess, enjoy music fountain shows, and enjoy a view of the Vilnia River.

The Bernardine Gardens can be found at B. Radvilaitės g. 8A, Vilnius 01143, Lithuania. You can visit it every day from 6am - 11pm.

Vilnius Cathedral

Over 80% of the Lithuanian population is Roman Catholic, explaining the abundance of landmarks and buildings with religious themes and influences. But the most visited, most important, and most beautiful place of worship in Vilnius is the Vilnius Cathedral. It was, and still remains, the center of Catholic worship in the city. It commemorates Lithuania's conversion to Catholicism, served as the coronation site of the Grand Dukes of Lithuania, and was also the burial site of many famous historic Lithuanian figures.

Vilnius Cathedral

Because of its striking neoclassical architecture, Vilnius Cathedral is in every tourist's bucket list. Visit this historic cathedral at Šventaragio g., Vilnius 01143, Lithuania.

8

Top Museums

You can walk the streets, see the views, and eat the food - but you can't really know a country until you learn of its past; what it grieves, what it takes pride in, and what it chooses to remember. To learn about Vilnius through its art and history, visit the following museums.

Museum of Occupations and Freedom Fights

(colloquially known as KGB

Museum or Holocaust Museum)

In line with the city's post-Soviet rehabilitative efforts, the Museum of Occupations and Freedom Fights was founded in 1992. It aims to commemorate the lives lost to the Soviet Union occupation and the Holocaust. Before the war, Lithuania had an estimated population of 250,000 Jews; but by the end of 1942, only 50,000 remained.

While it is understandable for tourists to want to skip something as bleak as remembering genocide victims, the experience would be nothing short of educational and eye-opening. It would also add depth to your experience by knowing that even after the most destructive event in modern history, the city and its people managed to survive, and even flourish.

You can visit Museum of Occupations and Freedom Fights in Aukų g. 2A, Vilnius 01400, Lithuania. It is open on Wednesdays to Sundays from 10am - 6pm. There is an entrance fee of €6, inclusive of audio guide.

Lithuanian Art Museum

The Lithuanian Art Museum is the country's largest and most visited museum. It is home to 230,000 paintings, prints, drawings, sculpture, and folk art. As a tourist, you might ask why you should visit the museum, when compared to internationally famous European countries, Lithuanian art is relatively unheard of.

What is especially interesting about the Lithuanian Art Museum is the historical influences behind the majority of its pieces. Throughout its history, Lithuania had been war-torn and oppressed. The art that arose as a response to prolonged persecution is proud, revolutionary, nationalist, and even romantic.

Every bit of freedom that they gained, they turned into art. Through art, they also illustrated the necessity of freedom, the sanctity of life, and the human ability to survive. The themes in Lithuanian art resonates to this day - across time, across language, and across cultures.

Visit the Lithuanian Art Museum at Didžioji g. 4, Vilnius 01128, Lithuania. It is open from Tuesday to Sunday, from 11am - 6pm.

National Museum of Lithuania

The National Museum of Lithuania, founded in 1855, is the largest collection of materials and artifacts pertinent to Lithuania's the history and cultural heritage. It currently houses more than 800,000 artifacts, assembled as exhibitions on archaeology, architecture, art, music, clothing, and more.

Visit the museum at Arsenalo g. 1, Vilnius 01143, Lithuania, any time between 10am - 6pm. It is open from Tuesdays to Sundays. Tickets cost €3 for adults and €1.50 for children and senior citizens.

Palace of the Grand Dukes of Lithuania

The Palace of the Grand Dukes of Lithuania, built in the 15th century, served as the residence of the country's leaders and nobility. Today, it has been repurposed as a museum and is also a venue for public events, performances, and exhibits.

Like many buildings in Vilnius, it is the result of combining many architectural styles. The tours aim to educate viewers about the palace's evolution from Gothic, Renaissance, to Baroque architecture.

The Palace is open every day from 11am - 6pm. It is located at Katedros a. 4, Vilnius 01143, Lithuania. Admission prices are €6 for adults, €3 for children and senior citizens.

Vilnius Museum of Illusions

The Museum of Illusions is a family-friendly museum that's sure to surprise the young and young at heart. It features artistic pieces that are designed to experiment with optical illusions, space manipulation, and visual humor. The museum's staff of friendly and informative tour guides will accommodate you and explain the exhibits as you go. Do take a lot of pictures! It is not only allowed, but encouraged.

The Museum of Illusions, located at Vokieciu g. 6, Vilnius 01130, Lithuania, is open on weekends from 10am – 9pm. You can purchase tickets online or at the reception desk for just €10.

9

Top Galleries

The 21st century marks the resurgence and the renaissance of Lithuanian art. If you're interested in buying art pieces, don't miss these five galleries.

Contemporary Art Centre

Founded in 1992, the Contemporary Art Centre houses the largest collection of contemporary art, with a focus on paintings, film, and music. The gallery has five exposition rooms, cinema, reading room, and a coffee bar.

The highlight of its permanent collection is the George Maciunas Fluxus Cabinet. Fluxus is an art movement by artists, poets, and composers in the 1960's. George Maciunas, its founder, intended to purge, or flux, the modern art world from elitism, classism, and commercialism.

Interestingly enough, the word 'flux' has another meaning, one that Maciunas also believed in. According to him, art is not a finished product, and it should not be treated as such. Instead, art is alive and should exist in a state of flux or 'non-art', as he called it.

The Contemporary Art Centre is in Vokiečių g. 2, Vilnius 01130, Lithuania. Exhibitions are open from Tuesday - Sunday, 10am - 8pm. Entrance fee is €3 for adults and €1.5 for senior citizens and children. Admission is free on Wednesdays. Check out their upcoming exhibitions on their website, http://www.cac.lt/en/exhibitions.

National Gallery of Art

The National Gallery of Art, founded in 1968, is a division of the Lithuanian Museum of Art. It aims to present 20th and 21st century Lithuanian art, with a focus on cultural heritage, history, and the universality of themes in Lithuanian art. The gallery also presents collections and exhibitions of notable Lithuanian artists such as Antanas Sutkus, Lev Antokolski, Petras Kalpokas, Valentinas Antanavičius, and Ferdinand Ruszczyc.

Visit the National Gallery of Art in Konstitucijos pr. 22, Vilnius 08105, Lithuania. It is open from Tuesday to Sunday, 11am - 7pm. Adults are charged an entrance fee of €2, while children and disabled people are charged €1.

Arka Gallery

In 1990, the Union of Lithuanian Artists founded the Arka Gallery in Old Town, Vilnius. The founding principle of Arka Gallery is that it does not discriminate against any art style, theme, trend, or concept; the gallery only intends to judge artwork solely on its artistic quality. The gallery's open-minded attitude towards art is especially encouraging for artists working with non-traditional media and materials. That said, expect eccentric exhibitions from artists like Augustas Bidlauskas, Gabrielle Helmke-Becker, Peter Rieder, Agnė Kulbytė, and Arūnė Tornau.

The Arka Gallery is located at Aušros Vartų g. 7, Vilnius 01129, Lithuania. Exhibitions are open from Tuesday - Saturday, 12pm - 7pm.

Vilnius Academy of Arts

The Vilnius Academy of Arts is the largest, oldest, and most reputable art university in Lithuania. The academy has five art galleries in Old Town, each with its own artistic focus, such as Artifex, which features post-modern textile artworks, and ARgenTum, which focuses on artistic jewelry.

Akademija displays visual art like paintings, sculptures, ceramics, and graphics. Modern and contemporary art exhibits are shown in Titanikas, while folk art and fashion exhibits are shown in Anastazija and Antanas Tamošaičiai.

Artifex
  Gaono g. 1, Vilnius 01131, Lithuania
  Open Tuesday - Saturday, 12pm - 5pm

ARgenTum
  Latako g. 2, Vilnius 01125, Lithuania
  Open Tuesday - Saturday, 12pm - 7pm

Akademija
  Pilies g. 44, Vilnius 01123, Lithuania
  Open Monday - Saturday, 12pm - 6pm

Titanikas
  Maironio g. 3, Vilnius 01124, Lithuania
  Open Tuesday - Saturday, 12pm - 6pm

Anastazija and Antanas Tamošaičiai
  Dominikonų g. 15, Vilnius 01131, Lithuania
  Open Tuesday – Saturday, 12pm – 6pm

Uzupis Art Incubator

An art incubator is an organization that aims to support, nurture, and facilitate artistic growth and development. The need for art incubators arose due to the modernization and commercialization of the art world. Art incubators aim to teach artists the necessary fiscal skills to be able to profit from their work. They believe that business, artistic growth and innovation are not mutually exclusive.

Such is the ethos of Užupis Art Incubator, founded in 2009. Today, it is considered the center of cultural and creative innovation in Užupis. The gallery features art exhibitions, live performances, and creative events.
  Visit the Užupis Art Incubator at Užupio g. 2, Vilnius 01200, Lithuania. It is open to the general public on Tuesday to Saturday, from 12pm – 6pm.

10

Top Restaurants

In Lithuanian culture, breaking bread is an invitation made in good faith. To feast in someone else's table is to also feast in their stories, culture, and traditions. That's why every traveller is encouraged to step outside their comfort zones and eat like a local.

Khachapuri Sodu

Khachapuri is a cheesy bread dish originating from Georgia. The bread has a well in the center which is then filled with melted cheese and eggs. The crust can also be torn and dipped into the center. Khachapuri, and other Georgian dishes like it, are served in Khachapuri Sodu.

Khachapuri Sodu may feel a little cramped, but the excellent food and warm service more than makes up for the limited space. The cosy restaurant is located just outside Old Town, making it an ideal resting place or a spot to get a quick bite to eat and a bottle of beer after a day of sightseeing. A meal for two people costs around €10.

Visit Khachapuri Sodu at Sodu g. 9, Vilnius 01313, Lithuania. They are open Monday to Saturday from 11am - 8pm.
+370 5 240 5851

Lauro Lapas

Take your palate on an adventure, too. Visit Lauro Lapas, a fine-dining restaurant perfect for those who want to indulge a little. The restaurant is dedicated to recreating traditional European dishes using the same ingredients, but with an ambitious, modern twist in technique and presentation.

From the outside, the restaurant may be unassuming, but once you step inside, Lauro Lapas is anything but. The atmosphere of the restaurant is elegant yet relaxed, and the waitstaff are attentive and accommodating. The menu changes every day, with the price averaging at €50 for two people.

Lauro Lapas is at Pamenkalnio g. 24, Vilnius 01114, Lithuania. They are open from 11am - 10pm from Monday to Friday. Please note that they do not serve food from 3pm - 5pm.

+370 610 01215

Lokys

The best Lithuanian restaurant in Vilnius is situated in a narrow road right next to the town hall. Restaurant Lokys has been serving traditional Lithuanian fare since 1972.

Its interiors are certainly unusual, to say the least. The restaurant is situated in renovated Gothic cellars. The original bricks and stones are preserved, which adds a sort of texture to the ambiance. They also offer outdoor seating in a courtyard, which can be quite beautiful in the summer.

Visit Lokys in Stikliu str. 8/10, Vilnius LT-2001, Lithuania. It is open on weekends from 12pm - 12am.

+370 5 262 9046

Gyvas Baras

Finding a vegetarian restaurant in a foreign country can be a hassle, but luckily, many restaurants in Vilnius are fit to accommodate dietary restrictions. Just one example is Gyvas Baras - they offer vegetarian, vegan, and gluten-free options at an affordable price point. The restaurant is famously known in town for their vegan falafels and burgers. Two people can feast comfortably for just €25.

Drop by Gyvas Baras at 11 Traku street 2 Pranciškonų street, Vilnius 01132, Lithuania. On weekdays, they are open from 11:30am - 11pm; on weekends, 1pm - 8pm.

+370 656 92939

Jurgis ir Drakonas

When travelling with family, eating out with kids can be a challenge - especially when they are unfamiliar with the local food. Fortunately, pizza is universally loved, even by the pickiest eater.

Jurgis ir Drakonas Pylimo is a family-friendly pizza place with five branches in Vilnius. Here, you can customize your pizza to suit your tastes and dietary restrictions. A meal for two adults and two kids costs about €70.

For the best pizza in town, visit any of the following Jurgis ir Drakonas branches:

Jurgis ir Drakonas Pilies
  Pilies g. 28, Vilnius 01123, Lithuania
  Open every day 11am - 10pm

+370 670 47146

Jurgis ir Drakonas Pylimo
  Pylimo g. 22D, Vilnius 01118, Lithuania
  Open Monday to Friday 11am - 10pm; Saturday to Sunday 12pm - 9pm

+370 600 77977

Jurgis ir Drakonas Ogmios
  Verkių g. 29, Vilnius 09108, Lithuania
  Open every day 11am - 10pm

+370 645 52250

Jurgis ir Drakonas Kaunas
  Kurpių g. 26, Kaunas 44287, Lithuania
  Open every day 12pm - 9pm

+370 672 00320

Jurgis ir Drakonas Akropolis
  07150, Ozo gatvė 25, Vilnius 08217, Lithuania (Shopping center AKROPOLIS, 1st floor)
  Open every day 10am - 10pm

+370 602 02035

11

Top Coffee Shops

Due to the recent tourist boom, the Vilnius food scene is rapidly diversifying and modernizing. And because Vilnius locals love their coffee, tea, and desserts, many coffee shops have also evolved to become more chic, more creative, and more experimental. Here are the top coffee shops to visit in Vilnius.

Chaika

In a city of pastel-colored buildings, the startlingly black facade of Chaika stands out. The interior, however, is much more comforting. You'll find white walls with grass-green accents, colorful tables paired with red chairs, and Soviet-era decor and artwork.

Chaika's drinks and pastries are vegan, vegetarian, and gluten-free. The menu includes coffee, tea, sandwiches, and cakes. Compared to other cafes on the same street, its prices are more affordable - a cup of coffee and a slice of cake only costs €5.

With Chaika, the search for the perfect brunch place is over. Head on to Totorių g. 7, Vilnius 01121, Lithuania anytime from 10am - 9pm.

Donut LAB

Donut LAB is one the city's newest dessert cafes. The interiors are well-lit, spacious, and Scandinavian-inspired. The family-friendly place serves colorful, delicious, and affordable donuts at just €1.35 each. The staff recommends the pistachio and crispy donuts.

For a quick sweet tooth fix, visit Donut LAB in Upės g. 9, Vilnius 09308,

Lithuania. The cafe is open every day from 10am - 10pm.

Crooked Nose and Coffee Stories

Crooked Nose and Coffee Stories is a few minutes outside of Old Town, but the artisanal single-origin coffee they serve makes it worth the trip. The cafe is well-lit and spacious, and the stark black and white walls is complemented by light wood furniture.

If you're unsure about what kind of coffee you'd like, just ask the staff! They would be happy to give you a crash course on the different types of coffee, beans, and brewing processes. The cafe also holds free coffee tasting events on select weekends.

Coffee connoisseurs, look no further. Visit Crooked Nose and Coffee Stories at Šaltinių g. 20, Vilnius 03213, Lithuania, from Thursday to Saturday. The café is open from 10am - 4pm.

Pinavija Cafe and Bakery

Pinavija Cafe is a chic, upscale family-friendly cafe and bakery. Its charming Parisian interiors attract tourists and locals alike, but it is an especially appropriate destination for those travelling with kids. There is a gated children's corner where kids can play with other children while the adults finish their meals.

Pinavija serves healthy sandwiches and pastries, made from all-organic ingredients. Vegans and vegetarians will find that there are plenty of options for them, too. Do try kibinai, a traditional Lithuanian pastry.

The location is a convenient breakfast place for tourists - the cafe is near many Old Town hotels, tourist attractions, and shopping district.

Pinavija Cafe and Bakery is located at 21, Vilniaus g., Vilnius 01402, Lithuania. It is open every day from 9am - 8pm.

Storytellers (previously Coffee1)

If you need to take a break while visiting Užupis, there is a coffee oasis located right in the middle of Uzupio Street. Storytellers is a laidback and cosy place with homey interiors. It has a view of the river, the Bridge of Užupis, and the famous mermaid statue.

The cafe is quite small and the seating is limited, but the food, service, and atmosphere is astounding. The atmosphere is particularly note-worthy - the servers are polite and prompt, and the owners are kind enough to check in and ask about your experience in the cafe and in the city.

Head on to Storytellers in Užupio g. 9, Vilnius 01201, Lithuania, open every day from 8am - 8pm. If you're coming in for breakfast, do try their espresso and avocado toast.

12

Top Bars

Meeting new friends, eating strange food, and drinking unheard-of beer - that's the perfect way to end a night in a foreign city. Here are the best of Vilnius' bars.

InVino

Invino is an upscale wine bar centrally located in Old Town, near different bars, nightclubs, and hotels. The cosy, vibrant bar is suitable for a small group of friends. In summer, you can request to be seated in the indoor terrace, which can be quite beautiful in the evening.

Invino offers an extensive wine selection at different price points, and should you need a recommendation, simply ask the friendly and informative bartenders.

For a relaxed night out, visit Invino at Aušros Vartų g. 7, Vilnius 01013. It is open every day from 4pm - 2am.

Spunka

If you're looking for a good old-fashioned hole in the wall, then you're in luck. Spunko is a small, unpretentious bar with an extensive menu of local craft beers. Seating is limited, however, as the bar can only accommodate 20-30 people at a time. Nonetheless, it's a great place to grab a drink or two after sightseeing in Užupis. It is also located near the Angel of Užupis and the Constitution of the Republic of Užupis.

Solo travellers and casual drinkers will love this bar. Visit Spunka in Užupio g. 9-1, Vilnius 01203, Lithuania. They serve drinks every day from 3pm - 11pm.

Peronas

Behind the Vilnius train station, there's an old, unused platform remodeled into a casual bar. It's a great option for those who don't mind train noises and loud music. For first-timers, it's recommended to get a table outdoors, where you'll have a nice view of the trains coming and going.

For a truly unique experience, grab a drink in Peronas. If you're lucky, you might even catch events like live music performances, slam poetry, and seasonal parties.

It is located in Geležinkelio g. 6, Vilnius 02100, Lithuania, open every day from 5pm - 4am.

Dėvėti

"Dėvėti" in Lithuanian means "used" or "second-hand". True to its name, the Dėvėti bar may look a little worse for the wear, but that only adds edge and character. It remains a vibrant, dynamic place with interesting interiors and a relaxed atmosphere.

Dėvėti is recommended for solo travellers looking to meet new people. It is an inexpensive, no-frills gastropub favored by locals and tourists alike. Their menu includes greasy bar grub like sandwiches, burgers, falafels, and potatoes. It is also one of the best dive bars in Vilnius that serve local craft beers.

Dėvėti is located in Lithuania, Sodų g. 3, Vilnius 01313, Lithuania. The bar is open every day from 3pm - 1am.

Alaus Biblioteka

Alaus Biblioteka, translated to English, means "beer library". The pub aims to make drinking a learning experience. Its walls are line with a multitude of beer varieties. German ales, brown ales, Celtic ales, American lagers, and Lithuanian beer – these are just some of the options, and we've barely scratch the surface.

The staff and bartenders are passionate and informative in all things beer. They also offer free beer samples to help you make your choice. Compared to neighboring bars, the prices are higher but still fair, considering that you're paying for the beer and the experience.

Beer enthusiasts should look no further. Alaus Biblioteka is in Trakų g. 4, Vilnius 01132, Lithuania. It is open from Tuesday – Saturday, from 5pm – 12am.

13

Top Nightclubs

At night, the Old Town experience completely transforms from cathe-drals to clubs, from cobblestones to dance floors. If you're interested in seeing the city's wild side, here are the five nightclubs you can't miss.

Loftas

Loftas is an industrial-style venue that hosts a variety of events, from concerts and live performances to fashion shows and cultural events. But on Friday and Saturday nights, Loftas becomes the city's premiere urban nightlife destination. Featuring various DJs like DJ Hell, D.A.V.E. the Drummer, dOP, and Metronomy, the nightclub attracts an interesting mix of hipsters and techno-pop fans.

Loftas is located at Švitrigailos g. 29, Vilnius, Lithuania. The nightclub is open from Friday - Saturday, 7pm - 2am.

Tamsta Club

If you're interested in live music, come and party in Tamsta Club. The place often plays hosts to a slew of concerts, small-time gigs, live performances, and the occasional stand-up comedy shows. Because of the variety in events and music, coupled with superb sound system and spacious dance floor, Tamsta Club attracts a diverse group of regular clientele.

It's located at A. Strazdelio g. 1, Vilnius, Lithuania, open Wednesdays to Saturdays from 7pm - 1am. You can purchase a ticket at the door or via their website, http://tamstaclub.lt/.

Baras Kablys

At first glance, you might think that the taxi driver dropped you in the wrong place. But inside this museum-like façade, is one of the city's hottest and hippest nightlife scene. Baras Kablys might be situated in an old formal palace, but its interiors were renovated to be as informal as possible. The culture bar features a skating park, hostel facilities, restobars, event halls, and dance floors. They also regularly host a variety of events like slam poetry, exotic parties, and concerts.

Visit Baras Kablys at Kauno g. 5, Vilnius, Lithuania. It is open every day from 11pm - 6am.

Cocainn

Just a few steps away from the Vilnius Cathedral is the eclectic nightclub, Cocainn. Staff and bartenders are friendly and accommodating, and are known to serve drinks with a bit of flair.

If you're looking to go clubbing with friends, Cocainn is the place to be. Do note that the doormen can be selective about the people they let in and that the bouncers don't tolerate rowdy troublemakers. Visit Cocainn in Gedimino pr. 2a, Vilnius 01103, Lithuania from 10pm - 5am.

Soho Club

Because of Lithuania's stance on homosexuality, not many LGBT safe spaces exist. That's where Soho Club comes in. It is a popular gay club that boasts an extensive cocktail list, spacious dance floor, flamboyant neon decor, and music by DJ Sonare and DJ Perfuro. Soho Club is an inclusive safe space where LGBT people can freely and safely drink, dance, have fun, and be openly affectionate.

Visit Soho Club at Švitrigailos g. 7, Vilnius, Lithuania. It is open on Fridays and Saturdays, from 10pm - 7am. Pro tip: if you can, try to avoid going before midnight. Soho Club only gets packed and interesting between midnight and 3am.

14

Only in Vilnius

Every year, a European city is formally recognized by the European

Union for its cultural diversity. For the entire year, the chosen city takes the center stage and becomes the newest 'IT' city and travel destination. In 2009, Vilnius was named as the European Capital of Culture. Since then, Vilnius has only gotten even more popular, attracting investors and tourists. It even made the Lonely Planet's top ten list of 2018 travel destinations.

Vilnius is an exciting, eccentric, avant-garde city that has a wealth of unique sights, activities, and experiences that you can only have there. By and large, Vilnius' most prized tourist experience is its neighborhoods, namely Old Town and Uzupis.

Old Town

Old Town is the most famous, most visited, and most beautiful neigh-borhood in Vilnius. It is also Lithuania's center of culture, religion, education, and politics; as a result, many tourist attractions are located in Old Town, such as the previously mentioned Gediminas' Castle, Cathedral Square, Three Crosses Hill, Church of St. Anne, and Gate of Dawn.

This central location makes it easy for tourists to visit a lot of them within a single day. Of course, if you're in no rush and would rather take your time in getting to know the city, taking things one day at a time is the best way to do it.

Here are some more unique activities you can do in Old Town.

· Visit Pilies Street, a short street right next to the Cathedral Square. It is packed with restaurants, cafes, flea markets, and street vendors. Here, you can do away with mass-produced keychain souvenirs and instead take home one-of-a-kind art pieces from Lithuanian folk artists.

- Old Town is a compact, walkable city with a plethora of churches. Meaning, if you're so inclined, you can visit the city's 28 churches and cathedrals in one day.

- Ride a hot air balloon over the city center. This is a must, especially if you're visiting during the summer or late spring. It's a once-in-a-lifetime experience that isn't cheap but certainly doable if you prepare for it in advance- a four-hour trip costs €200 for two people. For more details, visit https://orobalionai.lt/

- Frank Zappa is an eccentric American musician best known for his band's album, Freak Out! He's never been to Vilnius, but strangely, there's a statue of him right in the middle of Old Town. And nobody is sure why.

Frank Zappa Memorial
K. Kalinausko g. 3, Vilnius 03107, Lithuania

- On August 23, 1989, the world witnessed an extraordinary act of nationalistic resistance. Two million people, spanning three countries and 370 miles, held hands to peacefully protest the Soviet rule. It was the world's longest unbroken human chain, and it ended at the Stebuklas tile. Legend says that this particular tile has wish-granting properties. Simply stand on top of the tile, make a wish, and make a 360 degree turn.

Stebuklas Miracle Tile
Katedros aikste 1, Vilnius, Lithuania

- Literatu Street got its name from the Latin word 'literati', meaning people interested in literature. 19th the century, Literatu Street was populated by bookshop owners, writers, and poets. In 2008, a group of local artists wanted to honor their favorite Lithuanian authors, so they started decorating the first house in the street with literature-themed artwork. The Literatu Street Project, which has now expanded to cover the entire street, is a tourist's crash course in Lithuanian literature.

- Last but not least, do what every tourist does – shop. Large, upscale shopping malls like Akropolis and Panorama Mall are very popular in Old Town. However, if you're interested in a true Vilnius shopping experience, you should visit bazaars, flea markets, fairs, and street markets. Here, you can find inexpensive and interesting art pieces, jewelry, souvenirs, books, vinyls, memorabilia, antiques, and second-hand clothes. Brush up on Lithuanian currency and be prepared to haggle.

Akropolio Blusų Turgus
Ozo g. 25, PC Akropolis, Vilnius 08217, Lithuania
Open every Sunday, from 9am – 4pm

Halės Market

Pylimo g. 58, Vilnius 01136, Lithuania
Open from Tuesday to Sunday, from 7am - 6pm

Kalvarijų Turgus
Kalvarijų g. 61, Vilnius 09317, Lithuania
Open from Tuesday to Sunday, from 7am - 4pm

Užupis

Užupis is the city's artistic district. Interestingly, Užupis is an independent republic founded by twelve artists, complete with its own official flags and currency, a constitution, an anthem, and a 12-person army. In more ways than one, the new republic is a response to the Soviet occupation. In 1990, Užupis was a debilitating neighborhood - most of the buildings were destroyed, and those that weren't, didn't have basic utilities. The twelve artists rallied together to rehabilitate the city and restore it to its former glory, and today, it has become tourist destination open to everyone. Provided, that you're coming in with a smile. (Seriously. It's in the entrance signs.)

Here are some unique activities to do in Užupis:

- The Užupis bridge marks the separation of Old Town and Užupis, of tradition and creativity, of conservative and liberal values. In the bridge, you will be greeted with lover's locks, children's swings, and the famed mermaid statue. It is a delightful, quirky bridge that sets the tone for the republic you're about to enter.

Bridge of Uzupis
  Uzupio g, Vilnius 01200, Lithuania

Street art

- During your trip, take a minute to appreciate the street art, murals and graffiti; it is, after all, the city of artists. For more art like this, head to the Graffiti Pier, Vilnius River, and Pylimo Street.

- Should your visit fall on a Thursday afternoon, visit the Tymas food market. It's the perfect spot to try local delicacies, street food, and numerous healthy and organic vegan options. Alternatively, the Open Kitchen is open every Friday. It is like a weekly mini food festival that promotes the city's newest restaurants.

Tymas Market
 Aukštaičių g., Vilnius 11341, Lithuania
 Open Thursday, from 12pm – 5pm

Open Kitchen
 Aukštaičių g., Vilnius 11341, Lithuania
 Open Friday and Saturday, from 11:30am - 12am

· The official constitution of the Republic of Užupis is on public display in Paupio Street. The tongue-in-cheek republic, as expected, has a tongue-in-cheek constitution. It includes 41 articles. One article gives people the freedom to be happy or unhappy, if they so wish. Other articles aim to express more serious statements that the republic is built upon, like "do not give up".

Constitution of the Republic of Užupis
Užupio konstitucija, Paupio g., Vilnius 01201, Lithuania

· No one really knows whether the Republic of Užupis is a legitimate republic or nothing more than a really elaborate joke. But, as the old adage goes, "when in Rome, act like the Romans." Just go along with it and make the most of your visit. You can even get your passport stamped in a small craft shop called Užupio Kavinė.

Užupio Kavinė
Užupio g. 2, Vilnius 01200, Lithuania

15

3 Day Travel Itinerary

Medeina Statue – Old Town

Three days is not a lot of time to get to know a new city, especially one as unique as Vilnius. To help you out, this travel itinerary is designed to be four things: enjoyable, flexible, strategic, historically and culturally rich. It's supposed to be fun, dynamic, non-boring and non-repetitive. It's outlined to be action-packed but not too rigid that you'll rush through the sights. It's organized to minimize travel time by selecting the shortest possible route. And lastly, it's designed to be as meaningful as possible.

To get the most out of Vilnius, follow this travel itinerary.

Day 1: Old School, Old Town

From the airport, travel by train, bus, or taxi to your hotel. Get settled in, then explore the city, starting from Old Town. It's the perfect place to explore on your first day: the tourist attractions are only a few minutes away from each other, and you can travel by foot from one destination to another.

Start your trip with a visit to Cathedral Square, the most recognizable symbol of Lithuania. It's the central point of life in Vilnius: it is situated at the intersection of the city's main roads, and it's where many national events and festivals are held. Here, you'll find the Vilnius Cathedral, its Bell Tower, and the Stebuklas tile. During summer, there are also free walking tours

A two-minute walk south of the Vilnius Cathedral will lead you to the historic Palace of the Grand Dukes of Lithuania. The palace-turned-museum displays Lithuanian art, architecture, and archeological exhibits. After, walk through Arsenalo Street to get to the National Museum of Lithuania.

Next up is the Gediminas Castle Tower, which is a ten-minute walk from the Palace. The courtyard on top of the Gediminas hill offers a panoramic view of the city, which is also good a spot as any to wrap up the day.

Vilnius Cathedral, Bell Tower, and Stebuklas Tile
  Šventaragio g., Vilnius 01143, Lithuania

Palace of the Grand Dukes of Lithuania
  Katedros a. 4, Vilnius 01143, Lithuania

National Museum of Lithuania
  Arsenalo g. 1, Vilnius 01143, Lithuania

Gediminas Castle Tower
  Arsenalo g. 5, Vilnius 01143, Lithuania

Day 2: Historic City

Get ready for a crash course on the city's history, art, and culture. The second day of this itinerary includes museums, galleries, and historic locations. Begin the day in Vilnius University, the oldest university in the city. It is a world-renowned scientific center, architectural marvel, and art and cultural institution. Do visit their observatory courtyard, library, and the university tower.

Next, head on to the Museum of Occupations and Freedom Fights, previously known as the Holocaust Museum, Museum of Genocide Victims, and KGB Museum. It is a memorial museum that honors the victims of the Holocaust and Soviet occupation.

Take a break in the Bernardine Gardens, a public park with a view of Gediminas Tower, Bernardine Monastery, and Vilnia River. It's a picturesque and authentic park, ideal for families as well as hobby bird-watchers. Check out the alpinarium, rose garden, botanical exhibition, and the Belvedere hill.

For a mind-boggling, visually stimulating experience, head on to the Museum of Illusion next. Prepare to be dazzled with reimagined pop art, optical illusions, and riveting exhibits.

Lastly, to end the day with a dose of local art, visit the Lithuanian Art Museum. It's the country's largest and most diverse art museum, featuring almost 230,000 art and artifacts. Check out the museum's permanent exhibits on Lithuanian fine art, sculpture prints, folk art, and jewelry.

Vilnius Hill of Crosses

Day 3: Explore

On your last day, take the road less travelled, explore the city's streets, and discover its secrets. Start at the vibrant Pilies Street, where you can purchase souvenirs, clothes, ornaments, and folk art pieces. Pilies Street's extension is Didžioji Street, which is filled to the brim with luxury boutiques, souvenir shops, and novelty stores.

Just three minutes away from Pilies Street is Literatu Street. The houses in Literatu Street are lined with artworks, quotes, letters, trinkets, murals, and photographs, serving as an artistic memorial for famous Lithuanian writers and poets.

Next is a trip to the Užupis Republic, Vilnius' art district. Crossing the river, you will see the Bridge of Užupis and the Mermaid of Užupis. Walk through Užupio Street and take a right on Paupio where you'll find Constitution of the Republic of Užupis.

Finally, head on to the intersection of Subačiaus and Maironio Streets. Here, you can end the day with a picturesque view of the sun setting over Old Town and Užupis.

Conclusion

With its baroque beauty, rich history, and organic art and culture, Vilnius may very well be the last European city of its kind.

Many metropolitan cities like New York, Paris, and London often suffer from the pressure of being an internationally-recognized travel destination. They attempt to package the city into an easily digestible weekend experience, but often, the result is a diluted, expensive, gimmicky tourist trap. In pictures, the trip may look fun and cosmopolitan; but in real life, it's long lines, overrated food, and a very large bill.

Somehow, despite its recent fame and acclaim, Vilnius is immune to this phenomenon. It has managed to keep its small-town charm and humility, and this unapologetic authenticity is felt by everybody who comes (and comes back) here. In a world that is constantly looking for something new, Vilnius stands out by simply being true.

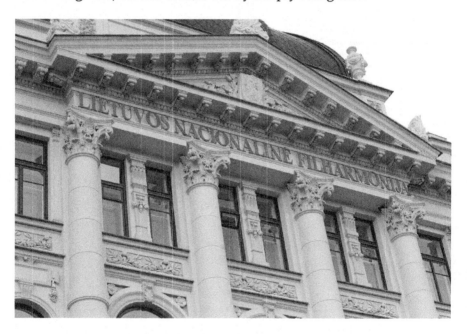

Thank You

I want to thank you for reading this book! I sincerely hope that you received value from it!

If you received value from this book, I want to ask you for a favour .Would you be kind enough to leave a review for this book on Amazon?

This document is geared towards providing exact and reliable information in regards to the topic and issue covered. The publication is sold with the idea that the publisher is not required to render accounting, officially permitted, or otherwise, qualified services. If advice is necessary, legal or professional, a practiced individual in the profession should be ordered.

- From a Declaration of Principles which was accepted and approved equally by a Committee of the American Bar Association and a Committee of Publishers and Associations.

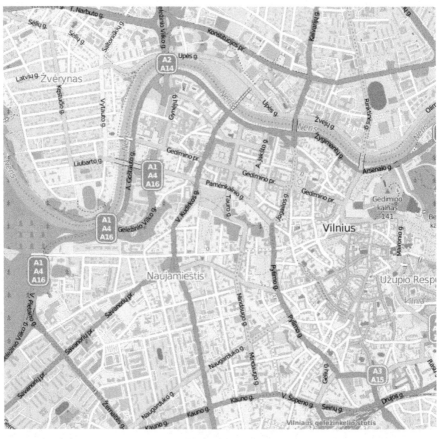

© *OpenStreetMap contributors*

Credit : https://www.openstreetmap.org/copyright